# Explaining The Anointing Of God

Bill Subritzky

Sovereign World

The Scripture quotations in this publication are from
The New King James Version. Copyright © 1979, 1980, 1982
Thomas Nelson Inc., Publishers

**British Library Cataloguing in Publication Data**
Bill Subritzky
Explaining the Anointing of God

ISBN: 1-85240-071-4

SOVEREIGN WORLD LIMITED
P.O. Box 777, Tonbridge, Kent TN11 9XT, England.

Typeset and printed in the UK by Sussex Litho Ltd, Chichester, West Sussex.

# DEDICATION

*To my dear wife Pat,*
*who has been such a faithful helpmate*
*over many years*

# Know The Anointing Of God

## What is God's anointing?

It is knowing the supernatural presence of God upon us. It is being aware of His presence with us. I would describe it as an actual physical experience when we feel the warm presence and glow of God upon our body. It is like a signal that God sends to us saying that He is showing His presence to us, that He is with us and approves of what we are saying or doing. With the anointing of God there is also the power and healing of God.

## Jesus Christ knew the anointing of God

> ...how God anointed Jesus of Nazareth with the Holy Spirit and with power, who went about doing good and healing all who were oppressed by the devil, for God was with Him. (Acts 10:38)

This describes how Jesus Christ ministered with the anointing of God. He was anointed with the Holy Spirit and with power and was thus able under that anointing to do good and heal all who were oppressed by the devil.

**The secret of the anointing**

The secret of knowing the anointing of God is complete obedience to His will. Thus we hear Jesus saying:

> *And He who sent Me is with Me. The Father has not left Me alone, for I always do those things that please Him.*
> (John 8:29)

Jesus Christ always knew the anointing of God because He always did the things that pleased God. We find that complete obedience to the will of God is the hallmark of His ministry:

> *He who is of God hears God's words; therefore you do not hear, because you are not of God.*     (John 8:47)

**With the anointing of God comes God's healing**

In the Gospels we have a clear picture of the anointing of God and the healing power of God. In Mark's Gospel we read the story of the woman who had a flow of blood for twelve years. She had suffered many things from many physicians and spent all she had, and was no better but rather grew worse:

> *When she heard about Jesus, she came behind Him in the crowd and touched His garment; for she said, 'If only I may touch His clothes, I shall be made well.'*
> *Immediately the fountain of her blood was dried up, and she felt in her body that she was healed of the affliction.*
> *And Jesus, immediately knowing in Himself that power had gone out of Him, turned around in the crowd and said, 'Who touched my clothes?'*

6

*But His disciples said to Him, 'You see the multitude thronging You, and You say, "Who touched Me?"'*

*And He looked around to see her who had done this thing.*

*But the woman, fearing and trembling, knowing what had happened to her, came and fell down before Him and told Him the whole truth.*

*And He said to her, 'Daughter your faith has made you well. Go in peace and be healed of your affliction.'*
(Mark 5:27–34)

Jesus Christ always knew the anointing of God and when it was falling around Him. He sensed immediately that some person was reaching out to Him and had drawn on that anointing. He could sense when it had happened and hence He was able to say 'Who touched my clothes?' although so many people were touching Him.

Many times I have been in a meeting when I have sensed the anointing of God falling like a shower from heaven. As the warmth of the Holy Spirit has fallen around me I have realised that somebody has reached out to God and that His healing power is touching their body. I remember one occasion when I was teaching on the anointing and a woman suffering from a stroke, who was sitting in the front row of the meeting, was instantly healed. As she believed the words of Scripture and the teaching on the anointing, the Holy Spirit was able to touch her. I felt the surge of the anointing falling and as I looked I saw her face and her body straightening as God's healing power manifested itself throughout her body. She stood up completely healed from her stroke.

Thus we see Jesus saying to the woman who was healed from the flow of blood:

*Daughter your faith has made you well. Go in peace, and be healed of your affliction.* (Mark 6:34)

7

## Raising from the dead

Such was the anointing with Jesus Christ that He knew He was able to raise the dead. We see Him taking the dead child by the hand and saying to her:

> 'Talitha, cumi' which is translated, 'Little girl, I say to you, arise.'
> Immediately the girl arose and walked, for she was twelve years of age. And they were overcome with great amazement. (Mark 5:41,42)

## When did this anointing come upon Jesus?

Jesus Christ did not commence His ministry until He was about thirty years of age. He did so immediately following His water baptism at which the Holy Spirit came upon Him like a dove. Many would say that this was when He was baptised with the Holy Spirit:

> Then Jesus, when He had been baptized, came up immediately from the water; and behold, the heavens were opened to Him, and He saw the Spirit of God descending like a dove and alighting upon Him.
> And suddenly a voice came from heaven, saying, 'This is My beloved Son, in whom I am well pleased'. (Matthew 3:16,17)

We notice that He was obedient to God, being led by the Holy Spirit into the wilderness to be tempted by the devil. There He fasted forty days and forty nights before His temptation. Following that experience He began to preach and say:

*Repent, for the Kingdom of Heaven is at hand.*

(Matthew 4:17)

He went about all Galilee, teaching in their synagogues preaching the gospel of the kingdom and healing all kinds of sickness and all kinds of diseases among the people. Thus He was able to say:

*The Spirit of the Lord is upon me,*
*Because He has anointed Me to preach the gospel to the*
*    poor.*
*He has sent Me to heal the brokenhearted,*
*To preach deliverance to the captives*
*And recovery of sight to the blind,*
*To set at liberty those who are oppressed,*
*To preach the acceptable year of the Lord.*

(Luke 4:18,19)

Because God had anointed Him, that is empowered and set Him apart for the work of the ministry, then the Spirit of the Lord God was upon Him. It was that anointing which enabled Him to preach the good tidings to the poor, to heal the brokenhearted, proclaim liberty to the captives, the opening of the prison to those who are bound and to preach the acceptable year of the Lord:

*And they were astonished at His teaching, for His word*
*was with authority.*                    (Luke 4:32)

The demons began to cry out with a loud voice saying:

*Let us alone, what have we to do with you Jesus of*
*Nazareth? Did you come to destroy us? I know You,*
*who You are—the Holy One of God.*       (Luke 4:34)

9

Many were healed:

> *Now when the sun was setting, all those who had anyone sick with various diseases brought them to Him; and He laid His hands on every one of them and healed them.*
> (Luke 4:40)

Demons also came out of many:

> *And demons also came out of many, crying out and saying, 'You are the Christ, the Son of God!' And He, rebuking them, did not allow them to speak, for they knew that He was the Christ.*
> (Luke 4:41)

Therefore we conclude that the anointing of God, that is the presence of the Holy Spirit upon Him, was an essential prerequisite to the ministry of Jesus Christ.

### Can this anointing be quenched?

Yes, we find that when Jesus came into His own country those who knew Him were offended at Him so that He could do no mighty work there with the exception that He laid His hands on a few sick people and healed them:

> *Now He could do no mighty work there, except that He laid His hands on a few sick people and healed them.*
> (Mark 6:5)

It was the unbelief of the people which prevented them from receiving prayer for healing. Their unbelief stopped them going forward for healing and hence they missed out on what God could have done through Jesus in healing them.

It is that same unbelief today which prevents many people coming forward and receiving a mighty healing. When people are prepared to believe that the Holy Spirit is with them as they are being prayed for in healing or deliverance then the anointing of God can fall. It is that anointing which breaks the yoke of sickness or demonic activity. It is God's presence manifest in a sovereign manner that destroys the bondages under which people are labouring. It is the magnificent presence of God Himself.

**Should we expect to know that same anointing?**

Yes. The Scripture says that the believer has an anointing from the Holy One and knows all things:

> *But you have an anointing from the Holy One, and you know all things.* (1 John 2:20)

This is an amazing statement. First it says that we have an anointing. The essential requirement for having that anointing is to believe that *you do have* an anointing. The second part of the statement says that we know all things. It is clearly referring to all things spiritual and as we know the anointing of God and know His presence, then we have a supernatural knowledge of things spiritual and a discernment and gifting which the world cannot know.

Further confirmation that we have the anointing of God comes from 1 John 2:27:

> *But the anointing which you have received from Him abides in you, and you do not need that anyone teach you; but as the same anointing teaches you concerning all things, and is true, and is not a lie, and just as it has taught you, you will abide in Him.* (1 John 2:27)

11

The teaching which is referred to here is not man's knowledge. It is the knowledge that comes only from the Holy Spirit who teaches us. When we have the presence of the Holy Spirit upon us, we have supernatural knowledge and do not need anybody to teach us about the anointing. It is the anointing of the Holy Spirit that teaches us concerning all things of the Spirit and through whom we know the gifts of the Holy Spirit, that is: the gift of the word of wisdom, the gift of the word of knowledge, the gift of faith, the gift of healing, the working of miracles, the gift of prophecy, the discerning of spirits, kinds of tongues, and interpretation of tongues.

It is the anointing through the Holy Spirit which opens to us all of the Scriptures and teaches us from the Scriptures concerning all things.

**How do we come to know this anointing?**

First of all we must understand the scriptural background of the anointing. The anointing in the Old Testament was a physical anointing with oil. God gave Moses the recipe to make up the oil with which the tabernacle of meeting, the ark of the testimony and all the utensils in the tabernacle were to be set apart or sanctified. The priests were similarly to be set apart by the use of this anointing oil. The making up of the oil is described in Exodus 30:22–30:

> *Moreover the Lord spoke to Moses saying: 'Also take for yourself quality spices—five hundred shekels of liquid myrrh, half as much sweet-smelling cinnamon (two hundred and fifty shekels), two hundred and fifty shekels of sweet-smelling cane, five hundred shekels of cassia, according to the shekel of the sanctuary, and a hin of olive oil. And you shall make from these a holy anoint-*

*ing oil, an ointment compounded according to the art of the perfumer. It shall be a holy anointing oil. With it you shall anoint the tabernacle of meeting and the ark of the Testimony; the table and all its utensils, the lampstand and its utensils, and the altar of incense; the altar of burnt offering with all its utensils, and the laver and its base. You shall sanctify them, that they may be most holy; whatever touches them must be holy. And you shall anoint Aaron and his sons, and sanctify them, that they may minister to Me as priests.'* (Exodus 30:22–30)

In due course Moses fulfilled these commandments as we see in the book of Leviticus:

*Then Moses took the anointing oil, and anointed the tabernacle and all that was in it, and sanctified them. He sprinkled some of it on the altar seven times, anointed the altar and all its utensils, and the laver and its base, to sanctify them. And he poured some of the anointing oil on Aaron's head and anointed him, to sanctify him.*
(Leviticus 8:10–12)

Thus it was that the tabernacle, all that was in it, the altar, the utensils and Aaron himself were set apart to the service of God by the anointing with oil.

In due course the sons of Aaron were also anointed because they were part of the priesthood:

*Then Moses took some of the anointing oil and some of the blood which was on the altar, and sprinkled it on Aaron, on his garments, on his sons, and on the garments of his sons with him; and he sanctified Aaron, his garments, his sons, and the garments of his sons with him.*
(Leviticus 8:30)

**Setting apart for service**

The anointing of God means being set apart for His service.

We find that not only were priests such as Aaron and his sons set aside for the service of God by having the anointing oil poured upon them, but also the same happened with kings. Thus we find that Samuel anointed Saul:

> *Then Samuel took a flask of oil and poured it on his head, and kissed him and said: 'Is it not because the Lord has anointed you commander over His inheritance?* (1 Samuel 10:1)

Saul was thus set apart as commander over God's inheritance among His people Israel.

The same happened with David when God chose him to be king of Israel. Again, Samuel took the horn of oil and anointed him:

> *Then Samuel took the horn of oil and anointed him in the midst of his brothers; and the Spirit of the Lord came upon David from that day forward. So Samuel arose and went to Ramah.* (1 Samuel 16:13)

We find that in the case of Saul, because of his disobedience to God, the Spirit of the Lord departed from him and instead of the Holy Spirit, a distressing spirit from God troubled Saul:

> *But the Spirit of the Lord departed from Saul, and a distressing spirit from the Lord troubled him.*
> (1 Samuel 16:14)

This event had happened because Saul had disobeyed God and broken His commandments. Because of that dis-

14

obedience God tore the kingdom of Israel from Saul and gave it to David. We realise that continued obedience to God is an essential element of knowing God's anointing.

## King Solomon

As King David was dying, he gave instructions for his son, Solomon, to be anointed king over Israel. Again we see the same procedure of the anointing, signifying setting apart for God's service:

> *Then Zadok the priest took a horn of oil from the tabernacle and anointed Solomon. And they blew the horn, and all the people said, 'Long live King Solomon!'*
> (1 Kings 1:39)

## The anointing of Jehu as king of Israel

We find that Elijah was instructed to anoint three people, namely Hazael as king over Syria, Jehu as king over Israel and Elisha, the son of Shaphat as prophet in the place of Elijah:

> *Also you shall anoint Jehu the son of Nimshi as king over Israel. And Elisha the son of Shaphat of Abel Meholah you shall anoint as prophet in your place.*
> *It shall be that whoever escapes the sword of Hazael, Jehu will kill; and whoever escapes from the sword of Jehu, Elisha will kill.* (1 Kings 19:16,17)

We see the fulfilment of the anointing of Jehu in the book of 2 Kings:

> *And Elisha the prophet called one of the sons of the*

15

*prophets, and said to him, 'Get yourself ready, take this flask of oil in your hand, and go to Ramoth Gilead.*

*Now when you arrive at the place look there for Jehu the son of Jehoshaphat, the son of Nimshi and go in and make him rise up from among his associates, and take him to an inner room.*

*Then take the flask of oil, and pour it on his head and say, "Thus says the Lord: 'I have anointed you king over Israel.'" Then open the door and flee, and do not delay'.* (2 Kings 9:1–3)

Following his anointing, Jehu acted with mighty power on behalf of God in destroying God's enemies.

### Similarly Joash was anointed king of Judah

*And he brought out the king's son, put the crown on him, and gave him the Testimony; they made him king and anointed him, and they clapped their hands and said, 'Long live the king'.* (2 Kings 11:12)

And again, Jehoahaz, the son of Josiah, was anointed king in his father's place:

*Then his servants moved his body in a chariot from Megiddo, brought him to Jerusalem, and buried him in his own tomb. And the people of the land took Jehoahaz the son of Josiah, anointed him, and made him king in his father's place.* (2 Kings 23:30)

### Conclusion

We therefore conclude that there is a clear pattern from the Old Testament of the anointing of priests, prophets and kings, such anointing being with the oil made according to the recipe which God gave to Moses, referred to in Exodus chapter 30 verses 22–30, quoted earlier.

This anointing with oil was a sanctification or setting apart of the person for God's service. It was a clear demonstration of the purpose of God in the setting aside of persons and things for His purpose. If the person disobeyed God then they were no longer under that anointing.

## Illustration of the anointing

We have an illustration of the anointing of God from Psalm 133. This is the picture of the precious oil made in accordance with God's instructions running down on the beard of Aaron and onto the edge of his garments like the dew of Hermon falling upon the mountains of Zion, where the Lord commanded a blessing:

> *Behold, how good and how pleasant it is*
> *For brethren to dwell together in unity!*
> *It is like the precious oil upon the head,*
> *Running down on the beard,*
> *The beard of Aaron,*
> *Running down on the edge of his garments.*
> *It is like the dew of Hermon,*
> *Descending upon the mountains of Zion;*
> *For there the Lord commanded the blessing—*
> *Life forevermore.*               (Psalm 133)

Thus the unity of the brethren is compared with the holy anointing oil.

**What about the believers?**

1 We live under the New Testament or New Covenant and have been called to God by His grace. We no longer live under the law but under the grace of God. However, the illustrations and types from the Old Testament are clearly applicable to us as believers today.

2 As we have seen from the Scriptures (1 John 20 and 1 John 27) we are anointed. We have received an anointing. Paul also confirms this in his second letter to the Corinthians:

> *Now He who establishes us with you in Christ and has anointed us is God.* (2 Corinthians 1:21)

Here we are clearly told that God has both established us and anointed us (set us apart in Christ).

3 How does this happen?
By being born again. Jesus said that unless one is born again he cannot see the kingdom of God:

> *Jesus answered and said to Him, 'Most assuredly, I say to you, unless one is born again, he cannot see the kingdom of God'.* (John 3:3)

When Nicodemus questioned him as to how a man could be born when he is old and enter a second time into his mother's womb, Jesus replied by saying:

> *Most assuredly, I say to you, unless one is born of water and the Spirit, he cannot enter the kingdom of God.* (John 3:5)

In order to be born again we must turn from our sins,

confess that Jesus Christ is the son of the living God, come to Him as a little child and ask Him to be our Lord and Saviour. We need to confess with our mouth and believe in our heart that Jesus Christ has risen from the dead. We must follow the commandments of God, namely to love the Lord our God with all our heart, with all our soul, with all our mind and with all our strength, to love our neighbour as ourselves and to love one another as Jesus Christ loved us. As we do these things, the Holy Spirit dwells within us and we are set aside, that is, sanctified and anointed of God. We are called to the service of God in the same way as the kings, priests and prophets of the Old Testament were called to that service.

4   We are priests and kings:

> *But you are a chosen generation, a royal priesthood, a holy nation, His own special people that you may proclaim the praises of Him who called you out of darkness into His marvellous light.* (1 Peter 2:9)

> *...and has made us kings and priests to His God and Father, to Him be glory and dominion forever and ever. Amen.* (Revelation 1:6)

From these scriptures we can clearly see that the believer is called to be a king and a priest in the kingdom of God.

5   Will God therefore anoint us?
Yes, because we are called to be kings and priests and are set aside for the service of God, then God's anointing will come upon us in the same way as it did upon Jesus Christ. In the Old Testament the anointing was a physical experience, as we have seen, that is, by the oil made up of specific ingredients (Exodus 30:22–30) being poured upon the kings, priests and prophets. In the New Covenant, however, the oil

is not a physical oil. The holy oil is the Holy Spirit of God which comes upon the believer:

> *For you did not receive the spirit of bondage again to fear, but you received the Spirit of adoption by whom we cry out, 'Abba, Father'.* (Romans 8:15)

When we come to Jesus Christ we receive the Holy Spirit of adoption. It is the Holy Spirit which anoints us and sets us apart for the service of God.


**The Holy Spirit is a Person**

He is not an 'it' but a Person. Jesus said he would send the Holy Spirit:

> *Nevertheless I tell you the truth. It is to your advantage that I go away; for if I do not go away, the Helper will not come to you; but if I depart, I will send Him to you.*
> *And when He has come, He will convict the world of sin, and of righteousness, and of judgment: of sin, because they do not believe in Me; of righteousness, because I go to My Father and you see Me no more; of judgment, because the ruler of this world is judged.*
> *I still have many things to say to you, but you cannot bear them now. However, when He, the Spirit of truth, has come, He will guide you into all truth; for He will not speak on His own authority, but whatever He hears He will speak; and He will tell you things to come.*
> (John 16:7–13)

He is the third Person of the Trinity and indwells the believer.

## Baptism with the Holy Spirit

An essential aspect to knowing the power of the Holy Spirit is to be baptised with the Holy Spirit. After His resurrection He breathed on His disciples so that they received the Holy Spirit:

> *And when He had said this, He breathed on them, and said to them 'Receive the Holy Spirit'.* (John 20:22)

Jesus Christ then told His disciples to wait in Jerusalem until they received the promise of the Father:

> *Behold, I send the Promise of My Father upon you; but tarry in the city of Jerusalem until you are endued with power from on high.* (Luke 24:49)

This command was repeated in Acts chapter 1:

> *And being assembled together with them, He commanded them not to depart from Jerusalem, but to wait for the Promise of the Father, 'which', he said, 'you have heard from me'.* (Acts 1:4)

> *But you shall receive power when the Holy Spirit has come upon you; and you shall be witnesses to Me in Jerusalem, and in all Judea and Samaria and to the end of the earth.* (Acts 1:8)

As they waited in the upper room, the Holy Spirit came upon the disciples:

> *Now when the Day of Pentecost had fully come, they were all with one accord in one place.*
> *And suddenly there came a sound from heaven, as of*

*a rushing mighty wind, and it filled the whole house where they were sitting.*

*Then there appeared to them divided tongues, as of fire, and one sat upon each of them. And they were all filled with the Holy Spirit and began to speak with other tongues, as the Spirit gave them utterance.* (Acts 2:1–4)

Peter explained that, having been exalted to the right hand of God, Jesus Christ had received from the Father the promise of the Holy Spirit which He had poured out. This was the explanation of the events on the Day of Pentecost:

*Therefore being exalted to the right hand of God, and having received from the Father the promise of the Holy Spirit, He poured out this which you now see and hear.*
(Acts 2:33)

I believe that if we really want to know the full anointing of God we must be obedient to this commandment of Jesus Christ and receive the whole promise of the Father by being baptised with the Holy Spirit.

If you wish to be baptised with the Holy Spirit, I suggest you say a simple prayer like this as you are upon your knees:

Dear heavenly Father, in the name of Jesus Christ, I renounce all my sins (name those sins) and I especially renounce all involvement in the occult or witchcraft on my own part or on the part of my parents or my ancestors. I renounce all fear and unbelief and any blockage of my mind. I ask you Lord Jesus to baptise me with the Holy Spirit.

You may be standing or kneeling. It is good to close our eyes and think of Jesus seated at the right hand of God ready to pour out the Promise of the Father upon us. As we quietly wait upon Him and allow Him to do this we begin to sense the peace of God. We should not listen to what we are saying but let God give us a new language.

## We must do something

God will not force us to do anything. Accordingly, when we are expecting to receive the gift of tongues which accompanies the baptism of the Holy Spirit we should be like a little child and open our mouths and speak out words. If necessary we can start with words which we make up. As we do so the cord between our mind and tongue is cut and our mind no longer controls all the words that come onto our tongues. As we become like a little child and are fools for Jesus Christ making baby-like sounds and continuing to have our heart directed towards God, the Holy Spirit will come upon our tongue and will give us the gift of a new language.

## The anointing is for today

We find that in the Old Testament the king, the priest and the prophet were anointed with oil which had a particular fragrance of cassia, myrrh, etc, and in this way they were set aside for the service of God. As they received this anointing, the power of God came upon them by the Holy Spirit and they were able to carry out great deeds by showing the power of God to His people. We have already seen from 1 John chapter 1 verses 20 and 27 that the believer has the same anointing by which we know all things through the power of the Holy Spirit.

## How do we feel this anointing?

We have read of the anointing oil being poured down on the head of Aaron and over his beard. Clearly he would have felt that oil as it was poured upon him. In the same way the believer can feel the anointing oil of the Holy Spirit as it descends upon him. This experience is for today.


## How to know God's anointing

1. Surrender absolutely to the Lordship of Jesus Christ.
2. Believe the Word of God in its entirety.
3. If you have never received any form of water baptism ensure that you are baptised in water, thus identifying with Jesus Christ in His death and resurrection.
4. Repent from all sin, especially unbelief, doubt, fear, things of the occult, unforgiveness, blockage of mind, wrong doctrine.
5. Be baptised with the Holy Spirit.
6. Read again the scriptures in 1 John 1:20 and 1:27 which confirm that we have an anointing from the Holy One.
7. Go on your knees and say a simple prayer such as this:

> Dear Heavenly Father, I come to you in the name of your Son, Jesus Christ.
>
> I praise you Lord and I worship you and I thank you that you love me so much that you sent your Son, Jesus Christ, to die for me and pay the penalty for my sins. I believe that I am reconciled to you through the blood of Jesus Christ and that I have received your peace. I renounce all sin, everything of the occult, all unbelief, all fear, all doubt, wrong doctrine, blockage of mind.
>
> These I renounce in the name of Jesus Christ and I ask you Lord to let me know that anointing which you

have already given me by the Holy Spirit. I confess that Jesus Christ is risen from the dead.

8. If you will do this with all your heart then you will sense the peace of God coming around you and you will feel the physical warmth of the Holy Spirit descending upon your body. You will know for a certainty the anointing of God as a physical presence of God upon your body. As the love of God begins to be shed abroad in your heart by the Holy Spirit, you will feel the physical presence of God around you or on some part of your body.

## The anointing breaks the yoke

We are clearly told from Scripture that the yoke will be destroyed because of the anointing oil:

> *It shall come to pass in that day*
> *That his burden will be taken away from your shoulder,*
> *And his yoke from your neck,*
> *And the yoke will be destroyed because of the anointing*
> *oil.* (Isaiah 10:27)

It is this anointing of God, the sense of His presence upon our bodies, which breaks the yoke of sickness, disease and depression. It causes demonic powers to flee.

## Blockages to the anointing

Sometimes I find that despite every effort on their part to know this physical presence of God, called the anointing, that believers still have a problem in sensing that presence.

In such cases I counsel the believer to be certain that he is honouring his or her mother and father and forgiving them of their sins. I then counsel them to renounce the sins of their parents and of their ancestors, especially any involvement in such occultic orders of witchcraft as Freemasonry, Druids lodge, etc, which block the anointing unless they are renounced. Past involvement in any form of the occult will, unless renounced, block the anointing. The same applies to wrong doctrine, fear, doubt, unbelief and unforgiveness. If, after having read this booklet, you still do not know the anointing of God I would counsel you to go through the occult checklist published in Appendix 1 and put a circle around anything in which you may have been involved and specifically renounce it in the name of Jesus Christ. You should do this with all your heart. As you do this you will know the anointing of God.

### Occasions of God's anointing

### *1. By the Word of God*
If we are to know God's anointing regularly and constantly we must be a disciplined reader of the Word of God. We should set aside part of each day for this purpose, preferably first thing in the morning. We should regularly read part of the Old Testament as well as the New Testament. We should ask the Lord to teach us by the Holy Spirit from His Word and to enlighten some part of the Word for us for each day. We must confess any doubt or unbelief that we have concerning the Word of God. The Holy Spirit will from time to time show us a scripture which we should learn by heart, and as we do this it can act as a breakthrough to the anointing of God.

## 2. Praise and worship

Where there has been praise and worship from the heart to God it is very common for the anointing to be sensed. We should enter His courts with praise, and as we do so and worship God, He makes His presence felt. It is not uncommon on such occasion, either during praise or worship or in preaching, for the anointing to fall upon some person or persons in the gathering and for them to receive their healing.

## 3. Salvation

The time when I know the strongest anointing of God in a meeting is when I make an altar call. As people come forward to give their lives to Jesus Christ in public and confess His name, I sense a powerful anointing fall upon the meeting. With the physical presence of God, the wind of the Holy Spirit often comes sweeping through the meeting. Many times I have seen people fall under the anointing without anybody touching them and others have been healed instantly as that anointing of God has fallen upon them. It is wonderful to behold the power of God. Recently, as the anointing fell on a meeting, I watched a man go rigid, his facial expression change and a powerful demon manifested out of his mouth before he was set free. The demons cannot stand the anointing of God!

## 4. When there is healing and deliverance from demons

When the signs following a ministry are occurring, such as physical and emotional healing, demons are being cast out and other New Testament occurrences are taking place, then the power of God's anointing falls continually in such a situation.

## 5. Testimony

When somebody is testifying concerning God's dealings in their life or of their healing or deliverance, an anointing will frequently fall upon their meeting.

## 6. Preaching the Word

When the preacher believes from his heart the Word of God and knows the power of the Holy Spirit in his life, particularly through the baptism with the Holy Spirit, then it is common for the anointing to fall in the meeting as he preaches. The preacher will himself know that anointing as he reads from the Scriptures and preaches the Word. It is as though he is receiving direction from God. Many times as I preach or teach I feel the anointing fall as though the Lord is saying, 'Yes, that is right, you are saying the truth, the right thing to my people.' It is like a radio signal to the pilot of an aircraft. As he hears the beep of the signal he knows he is on the right path. Similarly, as we preach the Word of God and teach in accordance with that Word, we should from time to time feel that anointing fall upon us, confirming that we are teaching in accordance with God's will. This is another way in which that same anointing teaches us concerning all things.

## 7. Using the gifts of the Holy Spirit

When the preacher is operating in the word of knowledge, the word of wisdom or discernment of spirits and the people sense the Holy Spirit's power present, then the anointing of God falls.

## 8. Prayer and fasting

Many times during prayer and fasting the anointing of God can be felt.

### 9. Walking in the will of God

When all our thoughts and actions are centred on God through Jesus Christ and we are seeking to follow His will, whether it be in the work place or elsewhere, we can frequently sense the anointing of God upon us. I often found during my business and legal career when I made a right decision that was pleasing to God, I felt the anointing of God fall upon me as though to say 'You have made the right decision.'

### 10. When two or more are gathered in the name of Jesus Christ

When there is a gathering of persons committed to the Lordship of Jesus Christ or who are seeking such commitment and who begin to put aside all doubt, fear and unbelief then the anointing of God falls on the gathering. This is particularly so at weekend seminars where people have been gathering together over the course of a day or two and have been living together in the same or adjacent premises.

As fellowship grows and the people listen to the preaching and teaching given by an anointed teacher, then the power of God can literally be felt in the place.

### 11. Repentance

As we have already seen, the anointing of the Holy Spirit seems to flow most strongly in meetings when there is true repentance in the act of salvation. It is an attitude of repentance towards God that enables Him to anoint us afresh with the power of His Holy Spirit. I recall one meeting where there was a large number of young people present and as I called them to repentance, many fell on their knees before God and confessed their sins. At that moment the mighty wind of the Spirit entered the building and the anointing of God fell. Afterwards many commented how they could sense a battle going on between the forces of good and evil as the Holy Spirit invaded the place with such anointing. As the anointing fell upon the meeting many people were instantly healed miraculously of various complaints, while demons came out of others, making loud noises and screams. Nobody present could deny that there had been a mighty visitation of God. As a result of this meeting and the power manifested in it, many people came to know Jesus Christ as their personal Saviour.

## Fragrance of the Holy Spirit

In every Christian gathering to which I speak I expect to smell the fragrance of the Holy Spirit. You recall reading from Exodus chapter 30 verses 22–30 that the holy anointing oil was made of various ingredients such as cassia, myrrh and sweet smelling cane. There was, therefore, a definite fragrance to that oil.

We find from Scripture that the same fragrance is upon the garments of Jesus Christ:

> *Your throne, O God, is forever and ever,*
> *A scepter of righteousness is the scepter of Your*
> *kingdom.*
> *You love righteousness and hate wickedness;*
> *Therefore God Your God has anointed You*
> *With the oil of gladness more than Your companions.*
> *All your garments are scented with myrrh and aloes and*
> *cassia,*
> *Out of the ivory palaces, by which they have made you*
> *glad.*                                    (Psalm 45:6–8)

We are promised that where two or three are gathered together in the name of Jesus, He is in the midst of them:

*For where two or three are gathered together in My name, I am there in the midst of them.* (Matthew 18:20)

I believe from experience and from Scripture that Jesus loves to manifest Himself in our presence and one of the ways in which He does so is through the fragrant aroma upon His garments. I recall one meeting in which an unsaved person came forward for salvation and in the counselling room he said he had never been in such a meeting. He thought that the singing was wonderful, and the prayers were good, but he told the counsellor that he just loved the perfume with which they sprayed the hall! I have known people to go from meetings smelling this fragrance around them for several days before they have realised it was the fragrance of the Holy Spirit. They have subsequently gone to a further meeting and been saved. It is a powerful witness of God's presence upon us.

Some people question the Scriptures in this regard. However, I accept these Scriptures without question. Those of us involved in the deliverance ministry know only too well the horrible stench that accompanies demons on many occasions. As demons are being cast out of people the stench often surrounds us. Thus we rejoice to know the beautiful fragrance of the Holy Spirit which comes upon us as we gather together in the name of Jesus Christ. The fragrance that surrounds the believer is a witness of His presence with the believer. This is how we are separated from the world. I believe also that the same fragrance from the Spirit of God can be among the believers when they gather in the name of Jesus and that this is a further expression of the meaning of the Scripture:

*Now thanks be to God who always leads us in triumph in Christ, and through us diffuses the fragrance of His knowledge in every place.*

31

*For we are to God the fragrance of Christ among those who are being saved and among those who are perishing.* (2 Corinthians 2:14,15)

## We need the anointing

If there was ever a time when we needed the anointing of God it is now. In the same way as Jesus Christ did not commence His ministry until the Holy Spirit came upon Him and anointed Him for service, so we need the full power of the Holy Spirit in our lives and this same anointing. From many years' experience in the healing and deliverance ministry, I have concluded that the greatest miracles of healing that I have seen have been when there has been a powerful anointing of God. The actual feeling of His physical presence upon my body and around the meeting has been the signal for great healings to occur. I have seen crippled people get out of wheel chairs, lepers healed, blind people see, the deaf and dumb hear and speak, strokes disappear, asthma go, cancer healed and every known form of disease disappear from people's bodies when there has been a powerful anointing. Oh, how I long for that anointing in the meetings, Paul said, 'Do not quench the Spirit.' All believers should know their inheritance in God and the anointing which He has already given them.

## Conclusion

We conclude that the anointing of God follows full and true repentance. If you have never known God's anointing then I suggest that you search your heart in every area of true repentance, renouncing not only your own sins in the name of Jesus Christ, but also the sins of your forefathers. In this way you are delivered from the curse of the law through the cross of Jesus Christ.

> *Christ has redeemed us from the curse of the law, having become a curse for us (for it is written, 'Cursed is everyone who hangs on a tree'), that the blessing of Abraham might come upon the Gentiles in Christ Jesus, that we might receive the promise of the Spirit through faith.*
> (Galatians 3:13,14)

I submit that past involvement in the occult either on our own part or of our ancestors can be a powerful blockage to the anointing. I further submit that failure to repent from sin, including failure to forgive and failure to renounce doubt, fear and unbelief, wrong doctrine and blockage of mind are all powerful reasons why we do not know the anointing. Further, I believe that in order to know the anointing we must absolutely believe that the Word of God is true from beginning to end and take it into our heart and not our mind.

Summing up, I would submit that it is when we earnestly seek the face of God in whatever circumstances and cast aside all doubt, fear and unbelief that His presence can be known physically to us as the anointing. On the other hand, where there is doubt, fear and unbelief in a meeting and it becomes strong enough, then the Holy Spirit can be quenched.

If we will do this as little children before God then we shall truly know His anointing. It may well be that we are called to prayer and fasting so that the bondages of the past can be broken under the anointing of God and we can really sense His anointing. It is true that we walk by faith and not by sight or by our feelings, but I am confident that if we do truly walk by faith then we shall know the feeling of the anointing of God.

May God richly bless you and anoint you!

# Occult Check Sheet

Place a circle around any area which applies. Before proceeding, bind Satan and the powers of darkness and loose the person's mind to the Holy Spirit so that he can recall things that need to be remembered.

### Have you been into
Witchcraft, Kabbala (occult lore), magic (not sleight of hand), blood subscriptions, hex signs, black magic (invoking hidden powers for bad ends), white magic (invoking hidden powers for good ends), hypnosis (whether magical or medical—it's dangerous), mental suggestion, mesmerism, self-hypnosis (self-induced trance states), Gypsy curses put on you (death, injury, or calamity), Pk (parakineses—control of objects by the power of the mind and will), Tk (Telekinesis—objects move around the room, instruments play, engines start...), black mass?

Do you carry an ankh (a cross with a ring tip—used in satanic rites, and dangerous)?

### Have you taken part with
Ouija boards, planchette (glass on the table), seances, mediums, floating trumpets, disembodied voices, etc, or consulted people who have clairvoyance (the ability to see objects or events spontaneously and supernormally beyond the natural range of vision—second sight) or clairaudience

(ability to hear voices and sound supernormally, spirit voices alleging to be that of dead people giving advice or warnings)?

### Have you engaged in
Activities involving mind reading, ESP (extra sensory perception), mental telepathy, thought transference, dream interpretation (as with Edgar Cayce book)? Or eckenkar or mind dynamics (Silvia Mind Control) or touch for health?

### Have you been into
Fortune telling by palm reading, tea leaf readings, phrenology (reading character, or one's future, by the conformations of a person's skull), crystal ball, cartomancy (using playing cards), tarot cards (twenty-two picture cards for fortune telling), handwriting analysis, numerology (reducing the letters of one's name to numbers), astrology and horoscopes, psychometry (telling fortunes by lifting or holding object belonging to the enquirer), transcendental meditation?

### Have you tried or practised
Divining, dowsing, or witching for water, minerals, underground cables, or finding out the sex of an unborn child using a divining rod, pendulum, twig or planchette. Also, the use of the pendulum, divining rod or a mechanical pendulum called a motor skopua for diagnosing illness and its treatment by colour therapy (using coloured threads) and 'screening' (using copper coils, etc)?

### Have you sought
Healings through magic practices using charms and charming for wart removal, death magic (where the name of the sickness plus a written spell is cast into coffin or grave), acupuncture, acupressure, conjuration (summoning up a

spirit by incantation), psychic healing, psychic surgery, concept therapy, or the use of a trance condition, or clairsentience (supernatural sense perception) or iridology (eye diagnosis to diagnose illnesses), sonarpuncture, radionics, astrologic medicine, chromatherapy, sound therapy, orgonomy?

### Have you participated in
Levitation (body lifting by demonic power), table tipping, spirit knockings, rappings, or automatic (spirit) writing, Hallowe'en parties?

### Have you been involved in
Yoga (exercises and meditation), karate, kung-fu, aikido, judo (martial arts), out-of-the-body (astral) travel of the soul?

### Have you been
Trusting in amulets (tigers claw, sharks tooth, horse shoe over the door), mascots, gold earing (man), talisman (magic picture), letters (occult) of protection, zodiac charms (birthdates) to compensate for lack of faith in God? Pagan fetishes (objects charged with magical powers and carried about as a means of protection or luck) come in the same category. Pagan religious objects, relics and artifacts which have been used in pagan temples or (pagan) religious rites, can be unknown to the owner, a focal point for evil influences in one's home, and should be burned.

   Omens, significant days, moon-mancy, chain letters and numerical symbolism, and so on, exercise an occult superstitious bondage over many lives and should be dealt with.

### Have you been on
Hallucinogenic drugs (LSD, heroin, marijuana, etc) or sniffing thinners, etc?

### Have you been into

Heavy acid rock (eg, Santana, Hendricks, Joplin, Deep Purple, Kiss, Black Sabbath, etc) or in the Jonathon Livingston Seagull sound track cult. (Such records should be destroyed.) Some paintings, posters, etc, done under hallucinogenic stimulus can be oppressive and evil.

### Have you visited

Pagan rites such as Voodoo (West Indies), Sing Sings (New Guinea), Corroborees (Australian Aboriginals), Fire Walking (Fiji, India), Umbahda and Macumba (Brazil), etc? Also visits to shows by Uri Geller or Matthew Manning demonstrating psychic powers could be dangerous.

### Do you possess

Occult literature? In particular such books as *The Sixth and Seventh Book of Moses, The Book of Venus, The Other Side, The Greater World*, the psuedo-Christian works of Jacob Lorber, and works by other authors like Edgar Cayce, Jean Dixon, Ruth Montgomery, Arthur Ford, Anton Le Vay, Dennis Wheatley, Eckhart and Johann Greber. Such books should be burned, regardless of cost (Acts 19:19).

Transference can take place through contact with a formerly occult involved corpse. Occult powers, oppressions, illnesses etc, have inadvertently been 'picked up' through contact in this way. Have you had any such experience?

1 Timothy 4:1 says:

> *Now the Spirit expressly says that in latter times some will depart from the faith, giving heed to deceiving spirits and doctrines of demons.*

The following is a list of cults and non-Christian religions which fall in the above category:

Jehovah's Witnesses (Dawn Bible Students), Mormons (Church of Jesus Christ of the Latter Day Saints), Herbert

W. Armstrong (Worldwide Church of God), Children of God, The Unification Church (Moonies, One World Crusade), Unitarian Church, Christadelphians, Freemasonry, Spiritualism, Scientology, Christian Science, Rangatuism, Religious Science, Anthroposophy, Theosophy, Rosecrucianism, Inner Peace Movement, Spiritual Frontiers Fellowship, Eastern Religions such as: Hare Krishna, Transcendental Meditation, Gurus, Divine Light Mission, Buddhism, Hinduism, Islam, Shintoism, Confucianism, Japanese Flower Arranging (sun worship), Bahai.

If you have enjoyed this book and would like to help us to send a copy of it and many other titles to needy pastors in the **Third World**, please write for further information or send your gift to:

**Sovereign World Trust, P.O. Box 777, Tonbridge, Kent TN11 9XT, United Kingdom**

or to the 'Sovereign World' distributor in your country. If sending money from outside the United Kingdom, please send an International Money Order or Foreign Bank Draft in STERLING, drawn on a **UK** bank to **Sovereign World Trust**.

## Sovereign World